Praise for *The Radical Practice of Loving Everyone*

*"I believe that animals are on the planet so that we can know love and compassion. We are profoundly connected to our pets more than we are usually aware of, and Michael J. Chase captures that love in **The Radical Practice of Loving Everyone**. I happily endorse this book!"*

— **Louise L. Hay**, author of the international bestseller *You Can Heal Your Life*

"I love this book! It's filled to the brim with gracious wisdom that's woven into wonderful, heartfelt stories. As you read Michael Chase's well-crafted words, you will find yourself laughing, nodding with pleasure, and even slapping your sides . . . as the gateway to 'loving everyone' opens wide and deep."

— **Denise Linn**, best-selling author of *Sacred Space* and *Soul Coaching*

*"**The Radical Practice of Loving Everyone** is exuberant, hilarious, and thought provoking. It is an observation of the qualities that earn dogs 'best friend' status and make us feel so good. More important, it's a reflection on how dogs can inspire us to be good, or at least better, human beings than we otherwise might."*

— **Anita Coupe**, chair, board of directors of
The Humane Society of the United States (2008–2012)

"I was in tears in the Prologue and laughing out loud in Chapter One. That's when I knew I was going to love this book! Indeed, Michael J. Chase has entertainingly captured not just the love affair we have with our dogs, but why we'd do well to give up self-help books and guru sessions in favor of studying our canines. Mollie is an utter delight, as are the lessons we learn from her through Michael's eyes."

— **Jeannette Maw**, master certified coach and founder of
Good Vibe Coaching